The Legend of Zelda: Breath of the Wild

Beginner's Guide

21st Century Skills **INNOVATION LIBRARY**

Josh Gregory

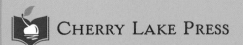

Published in the United States of America by Cherry Lake Publishing Group
Ann Arbor, Michigan
www.cherrylakepublishing.com

Reading Adviser: Beth Walker Gambro, MS, Ed., Reading Consultant, Yorkville, IL

Cherry Lake Press is an imprint of Cherry Lake Publishing Group.

Library of Congress Cataloging-in-Publication Data

Names: Gregory, Josh, author.
Title: The legend of Zelda : beginner's guide / by Josh Gregory.
Description: Ann Arbor, Michigan : Cherry Lake Publishing, 2022. | Series:
  Unofficial guides | Includes bibliographical references and index. |
  Audience: Grades 4-6 | Summary: "The Legend of Zelda: Breath of the Wild
  offers players a wide-open world of action and adventure where they can
  explore endlessly and tackle goals in any order. The tips and hints in
  this book will give players everything they need to uncover the game's
  deepest secrets and defeat its toughest enemies. Includes table of
  contents, author biography, sidebars, glossary, index, and informative
  backmatter"— Provided by publisher.
Identifiers: LCCN 2021042786 (print) | LCCN 2021042787 (ebook) | ISBN
  9781534199729 (library binding) | ISBN 9781668900864 (paperback) | ISBN
  9781668902301 (ebook) | ISBN 9781668906620 (pdf)
Subjects: LCSH: Legend of Zelda (Game)—Juvenile literature.
Classification: LCC GV1469.35.L43 G74 2022 (print) | LCC GV1469.35.L43
  (ebook) | DDC 794.8—dc23
LC record available at https://lccn.loc.gov/2021042786
LC ebook record available at https://lccn.loc.gov/2021042787

Cherry Lake Publishing Group would like to acknowledge the work of the Partnership for 21st Century Learning, a Network of Battelle for Kids. Please visit http://www.battelleforkids.org/networks/p21 for more information.

Printed in the United States of America
Corporate Graphics

Josh Gregory is the author of more than 125 books for kids. He has written about everything from animals to technology to history. A graduate of the University of Missouri–Columbia, he currently lives in Chicago, Illinois.

Contents

CHAPTER 1

New Directions

The Legend of Zelda: Breath of the Wild has a larger world and more freedom to explore than any previous *Zelda* game. Its main themes are wilderness exploration and survival. This means players need to gather supplies, **craft** useful items, and even pay attention to the weather as they adventure through the world of Hyrule.

When you start *Breath of the Wild* for the first time, you'll find Link waking up from a deep sleep. This is the way every game in the main *Legend of Zelda* series begins. But this time, Link has been taking an especially long nap. You'll soon discover that he has been asleep for 100 years! A lot has changed in the world, and it will be up to you to discover what happened in Link's past and during the time he was asleep.

There is a lot for new players to learn about *Breath of the Wild*. Luckily, the game's opening section does a great job of explaining the basics. As Link wakes up, you'll start receiving messages from a mysterious voice. Do as it says and head out of the chamber. Inside some wooden chests in the next hallway, you'll find some basic clothes to put on. Keep going and you'll find yourself in a big open area called the Great **Plateau**. Though the plateau is large, it is only a small part of the enormous world you'll get to explore. If you want to see the rest, you'll have to complete a few tasks first. These

You'll start out with almost no gear when you first arrive on the Great Plateau.

A Big Game Gets Even Bigger

The Legend of Zelda: Breath of the Wild is a massive adventure. If you want to see everything in the game, you'll need to spend dozens or possibly hundreds of hours playing. But dedicated players will eventually run out of things to do in even the biggest games.

A few months after the game's release, Nintendo began releasing additional content for players who couldn't get enough *Zelda*. By purchasing an Expansion Pass, players got everything from new weapons and armor to new quests and even a harder difficulty mode. This helped ensure that even the most active players could go a long time without running out of things to do!

will grant you useful abilities and teach you how to play the game.

First, the mysterious voice will tell you to make use of Link's Sheikah Slate. This handy device looks somewhat like a Nintendo Switch, and you will use it for all kinds of things throughout the game. Pulling it out for the first time on the plateau will lead you to a machine where you can connect your Sheikah Slate. This causes a tall tower to rise up out of the ground and lift you high into

Towers are great places to get a view of your surroundings.

the sky. You'll also see a scene that gives you a little more background info on what is happening in the world.

Climb down from the tower and you'll run into an old man. You may already have met him if you explored the plateau a little before following the voice's instructions. The old man will tell you to visit four **shrines** on the plateau. Shrines are an important part of *Breath of the Wild*. Each one contains puzzles or a combat challenge. Overcoming these obstacles will grant you important rewards. Completing the first four shrines on the Great Plateau will give you access to Link's special rune abilities. The Remote Bomb rune lets you place bombs and set them off from a distance. The Magnesis rune lets you grab and move metal objects. The Stasis rune lets you briefly stop time for a moving object. Finally, the Cryonis rune lets you turn water into ice. These four runes are necessary to solve puzzles throughout *Breath of the Wild*. You can also use them to defeat enemies and reach new locations as you are out exploring the world.

Once you have the Remote Bomb rune, you'll always have a way to blow up rocks, attack enemies, and more.

Gliding is one of the most important skills in *Breath of the Wild*. You can cross huge distances very quickly if you start from a high enough position.

Once you have completed the four shrines on the plateau and unlocked the rune abilities, the old man will give you one more important tool: a paraglider. You can open this glider anytime Link is in the air. It will let you fall safely from great heights or sail from one tall point to another. You'll use it constantly during your adventure. But for now, it has one especially important use: you can open it up to safely glide down from the Great Plateau into the wide-open world of Hyrule!

CHAPTER 2

A Wide-Open World

Now that you are off the Great Plateau and equipped with your most important abilities, all of Hyrule is available to explore. From the highest mountain peak to the most distant lands, every single place you can see can be reached. Sometimes you might need to be creative to overcome obstacles. But the game will never tell you that a location is off-limits.

You can use several different types of movement to make your way across Hyrule. The most basic is to simply walk or jog by pressing the left control stick in any direction. If you hold down the B button while doing this, you can also sprint. If you move toward a wall, mountain, or other vertical surface, Link can climb upward. Almost everything in the game can be climbed, though there are sometimes special walls that prevent it. Finally, you can swim by jumping into a body of water. However, you can only swim along the surface, rather than diving underwater.

Aside from basic walking and jogging, all of these movement actions require **stamina**. Anytime you are doing something that requires stamina, a green wheel will pop up on screen. This wheel will slowly decrease as Link uses up stamina. When it reaches zero, Link will be tired out. If you are climbing, he will fall down. If you are swimming, he will sink. Using your paraglider also

The stamina wheel will pop up anytime you start sprinting.

takes up stamina. This means you can't glide across the entire map all at once.

To restore stamina, simply find a place to pause and rest on flat land. The wheel will slowly fill back up. This means you need to plan your movements carefully

Before climbing a cliff like this, plan out the points where you will be able to pause and regain stamina.

when exploring. Want to climb a tall mountain? Find a path where you can stop to rest on ledges every so often. Need to cross a wide river? Look for islands or rocks you can rest on as you swim across. Finding and

Keep an Eye on the Environment

You'll need to cross all kinds of different environments on your journey through Hyrule. There are sprawling, sandy deserts and snowy mountaintops. There are tropical beaches and thick, green forests. There are even bustling towns where you'll meet a variety of colorful characters. Each of these places has its own unique challenges and risks. In icy areas, you'll freeze without the proper clothing. Under the hot desert sun, you'll need to find ways to stay cool.

Everything from the time of day to the current weather will affect your travels. You'll need to pay close attention and be ready to change your plans at a moment's notice if necessary. For example, you might get caught off guard by a thunderstorm as you are climbing a cliff wall. The rain will make the wall slippery. Worse yet, lightning could strike you if you are wearing any metal items. You'll need to find a safe place to take shelter until the storm passes.

planning a route to get where you want to go is a big part of the challenge in *Breath of the Wild*. Be creative, and don't be afraid to try weird things when you are trying to reach a far-off area.

Sometimes you might want to cross a long distance as fast as possible. With such a huge world, it can take a long time to get from one place to another, even if there are no obstacles in the way. Luckily, you don't have to travel everywhere on foot. If you want a faster ride, you can tame a wild horse. You'll find these

Each horse has a different appearance and different abilities. Find one that you like and stick with it for a while to improve it.

creatures wandering all over the fields of Hyrule. Sneak up on one from behind and press the A button when prompted to jump on its back. The horse will start jumping around, trying to knock you off its back. You'll need to tap the L button quickly to settle the horse down before you run out of stamina. Once you tame a horse, you can take it to a **stable**. These buildings are spread out across Hyrule, often near towns. There, you can register the horse, name it, and give it a saddle. From then on, you'll be able to summon the horse from any stable. You can have up to five different horses registered at a time.

Hyrule is a huge place. Thankfully, your Sheikah Slate has a handy map that you can access at any time. At first, it will only show part of the world. To fill in the rest, you'll need to visit more towers like the one you found on the Great Plateau. As you visit towers and other major locations, they will automatically be marked on your map. Afterward, you can open the map at any time and instantly travel to these points from anywhere in the world. You can also click the right stick at any time to use your Sheikah Slate as a scope that lets you zoom in. While looking through the scope, you can press the A button to mark locations you want to explore. This will mark them on your map so you can plan the best way to reach your goal.

CHAPTER 3

Survival Skills

Hyrule is beautiful, but it can be a dangerous place. All kinds of enemies roam through the wilderness. Some of them are very easy to deal with. Others offer a serious challenge to even the most seasoned explorers.

Breath of the Wild gives players a huge range of options for dealing with enemies. The simplest is to attack them head-on. There are all kinds of weapons you can find and use against your foes, from swords and axes to spears and magic wands. Sometimes you will find these weapons in treasure chests or lying on the ground. Other times, enemies will drop them. There are also special weapons that can only be won by completing special quests.

You can carry many weapons at once and switch between them at any time. This is a good thing, because every weapon you find will eventually break after you use it enough. Different weapons have different amounts of **durability**. Some will break after a few swings, while others can last for quite a while. This means you need to constantly find and pick up new weapons as you go. You don't want to be caught empty-handed in a fight!

Different kinds of weapons handle differently in combat. For example, Link will move more slowly when

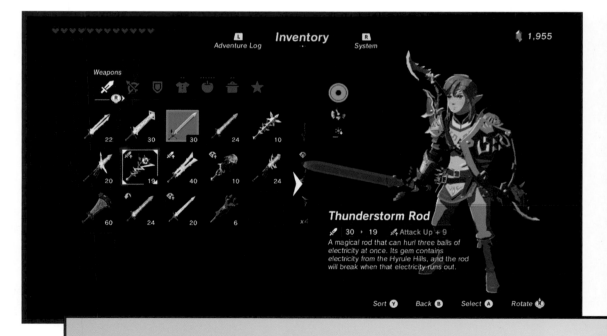

It's good to try and carry as wide a variety of weapons as possible so you will be prepared for any situation.

swinging a big, heavy weapon. Experiment with different weapons to see which ones work best with your play style.

Some weapons work best against certain types of enemies. For example, a big, heavy axe might help you break through an armored enemy's defenses. A fast sword might be better for dealing with small, nimble foes. Some enemies have specific weaknesses. For example, you might find a weapon that has fire, ice, or electric powers. You'll also run into enemies that are

Making Money

Money in *Breath of the Wild* comes in the form of rupees. Rupees are useful for buying things from shops, upgrading your gear, and more. You can earn them in all kinds of ways. Sometimes you might find them in treasure chests or get them as rewards for completing quests. But one of the best ways to make money fast is to cook a lot of food and sell it at shops. Cooked food sells for much more than uncooked ingredients.

When you are locked on to an enemy, a red-orange arrow will appear above their head.

weak against fire, ice, or electric. Using the correct weapon against them will do extra damage.

When a battle starts, hold the ZL button to lock the game's camera to the nearest enemy. This will make it easier for you to move around as you fight. Stay in motion and watch your enemy closely to avoid attacks. If you have a shield, Link will hold it up as you hold ZL. This will help you block attacks. Be careful though.

Shields can break just like weapons! As you hold ZL, press the X button to jump or dodge in whatever direction you are moving. If you time your dodges just right, you can avoid most attacks. You might even get the perfect chance for a powerful counterattack.

Press the A button just as an enemy's attack is about to hit you. If you time it right, you will swing your shield, knock the enemy back, and stun the enemy so you can strike back.

You will also find bows and arrows throughout Hyrule. These allow you to attack from a distance. You can aim your bow at any time by holding down the ZR button. You can only fire if you have arrows to spare. Also, bows will eventually break just like other weapons. If you're out of arrows and need to make a ranged attack, you can also throw your regular weapon at enemies by holding the R button. Remember to pick it up again after you throw it!

When you are aiming your bow, a small number near your target will show how many arrows you have left.

It can be fun to use your scope to watch what enemies do when they can't see you.

It's usually best not to go running straight into a fight. Instead, use your scope to look around and see where enemies are located. Plan your attack carefully. Then sneak up and get the jump on your foes. Click the left stick to make Link crouch. Then move slowly and stay out of sight. Enemies won't notice you until they see or hear you. In the bottom-right corner, there is a meter that shows how noisy you are being. If an enemy notices something, a question mark will pop up above its head. At this point, you still have a chance to hide.

But if the question mark becomes an exclamation point, you've been spotted.

Remember that enemies can be hurt by all the same things that are dangerous to Link. If you look around, you can usually find creative ways to attack using the environment. Are some enemies standing near the bottom of a hill? Try pushing a boulder so it rolls down and hits them. Are they standing in a dry, grassy field? Set the field on fire! You can also use your rune abilities against enemies. See a metal crate nearby? Use Magnesis to pick it up and drop it on your enemy. There is a lot of room for creativity. Use your imagination and don't be afraid to try new things in battle.

When you begin the game, you'll have no items or equipment. Link doesn't even have clothes to wear at first! Thankfully, there are all kinds of useful items to find as you play. Different types of clothing can really come in handy. Some items give you more protection from enemy attacks. Others make you better at climbing, sneaking, or other actions. Some gear will also make it easier to deal with harsh weather conditions. Seek out new clothing by visiting shops, opening treasure chests, and completing quests.

In such a dangerous environment, Link is bound to take some damage from time to time. To heal, all he needs to do is eat. There are all kinds of foods scattered in the wild, from fruit and vegetables to

Many food items can be found just laying on the ground around Hyrule.

Different combinations of ingredients will create different dishes for Link to eat.

meat and seasonings. You can collect these items and use them to prepare various recipes. Up to five different ingredients can go into each recipe. Each dish heals Link for a different number of hearts. Some also have other benefits, such as increasing defense or attack power for a short time. To prepare food, bring ingredients to a cooking pot. You'll find these all over Hyrule, usually near towns, stables, and other settlements.

CHAPTER 4

Getting Things Done

Breath of the Wild is a very open-ended game. You don't have to complete anything in any specific order. If you are brave, you can even head straight to the game's final battle right after leaving the plateau! However, it's worth it to spend time completing the game's other goals first. Each one will help Link grow stronger and provide useful new abilities. Completing various goals will also help you learn more about the story and discover everything that happened while Link was asleep.

One of the main goals of the game's story is to discover and activate four giant mechanical creatures called Divine Beasts. It takes a lot of careful exploration and puzzle solving to get inside each Divine Beast. Once you're there, you'll face off against even more puzzles and some especially tough enemies. But for each

Divine Beast you activate, you'll get a very useful new ability. You'll also weaken the game's final enemy a bit, making the last battle slightly easier.

Another major goal is to seek out shrines like the ones you completed before leaving the Great Plateau. There are 120 shrines hidden throughout Hyrule. Some are easy to find, while others are cleverly hidden away. Each shrine contains a short set of puzzles or combat

Shrines are covered in glowing blue lights, so you can often spot them from a distance. Some are well-hidden, though.

challenges. Completing these will grant you items called Spirit Orbs. Spirit Orbs are very important if you want Link to get stronger. You can take them to Goddess Statues, which are found in some of Hyrule's major locations. For each four Spirit Orbs you give a Goddess Statue, you can increase either health or stamina. The more shrines you complete, the more damage Link can take and the easier it is to travel around.

The Next Adventure

At the 2019 Electronic Entertainment Expo, Nintendo showed off a trailer for the next *Legend of Zelda* game. Fans were thrilled to see that the new game would be a direct sequel to *Breath of the Wild*. It is planned to carry on the same exploration and survival themes *Breath of the Wild* introduced to the series, though there are sure to be some surprising new changes. Not much other information is known about the new game yet, but fans are eagerly awaiting more news of the next *Zelda* adventure.

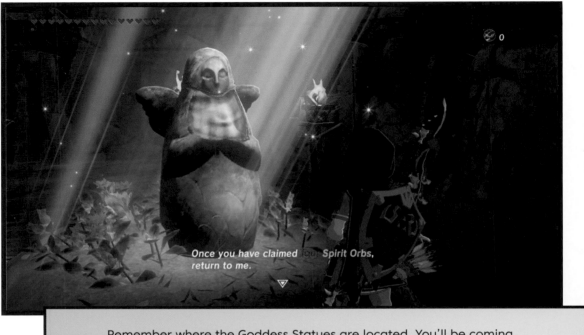

Once you have claimed four Spirit Orbs, return to me.

Remember where the Goddess Statues are located. You'll be coming back to them often as you complete shrines.

Throughout Hyrule, there are certain locations that will trigger Link's lost memories of the past. Various characters can offer you clues to help find these locations. When you do, you'll see glowing points that you can approach to trigger scenes. Finding these locations is highly recommended if you want to know what's going on in the story!

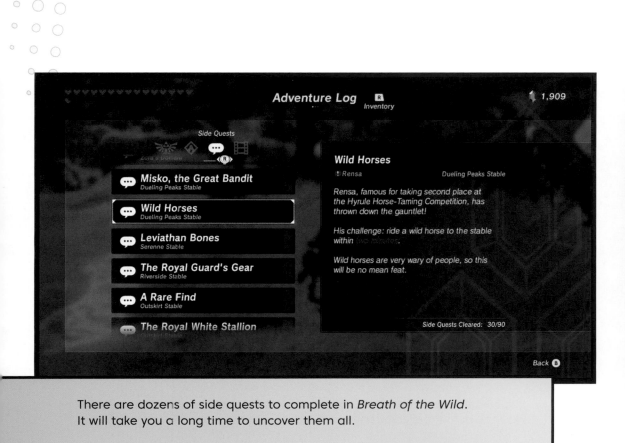

Adventure Log 🄡
Inventory

🔺 1,909

Side Quests

Wild Horses

💬 Misko, the Great Bandit
Dueling Peaks Stable

💬 Wild Horses
Dueling Peaks Stable

💬 Leviathan Bones
Serenne Stable

💬 The Royal Guard's Gear
Riverside Stable

💬 A Rare Find
Outskirt Stable

💬 The Royal White Stallion

Wild Horses
💬 Rensa   Dueling Peaks Stable

Rensa, famous for taking second place at
the Hyrule Horse-Taming Competition, has
thrown down the gauntlet!

His challenge: ride a wild horse to the stable
within two minutes.

Wild horses are very wary of people, so this
will be no mean feat.

Side Quests Cleared: 30/90

Back 🅑

There are dozens of side quests to complete in *Breath of the Wild*.
It will take you a long time to uncover them all.

You'll also run into all kinds of side quests as you
explore. Most of them begin when characters ask you
to do things or give you hints about Hyrule's secrets.
Completing these quests is a great way to unlock
unique weapons and gear, make money, and more.

Need a handy way to keep track of your progress in the
game's many goals? Open up the Adventure Log on
Link's Sheikah Slate. It automatically keeps track of
which things you've done. It also reminds you of any

clues or hints you've uncovered so far. It can even mark locations on your map so you know where to go next.

Whenever you feel ready, you can tackle the final challenge of *Breath of the Wild*: Hyrule Castle. Located right in the center of the map, this castle is guarded by some of the toughest enemies in the game. Deep inside it, you will find the evil Calamity Ganon. Defeating him could be what it takes to save the world. Are you ready to do it?

Even after you conquer Hyrule Castle and defeat Calamity Ganon, there is still plenty to do in *Breath of the Wild*. Even if you manage to complete every shrine and uncover all of Link's memories, there is always more gear to find and new places to discover. Best of all, you can set your own challenges and enjoy the fun of wandering Hyrule. Happy adventuring!

GLOSSARY

craft (KRAFT) to make something

durability (dur-uh-BIL-uh-tee) an object's ability to be used without wearing out or breaking

plateau (pla-TOW) a raised, flat area of land

shrines (SHRYNZ) special places built to remember or celebrate something

stable (STAY-buhl) a place where horses are kept and cared for

stamina (STA-mih-nuh) a person or animal's ability to do something for a long time without resting

FIND OUT MORE

Books

Cunningham, Kevin. *Video Game Designer*. Ann Arbor, MI: Cherry Lake Publishing, 2016.

Loh-Hagan, Virginia. *Video Games*. Ann Arbor, MI: Cherry Lake Publishing, 2021.

Powell, Marie. *Asking Questions About Video Games*. Ann Arbor, MI: Cherry Lake Publishing, 2016.

Websites

The Legend of Zelda: Breath of the Wild
www.zelda.com/breath-of-the-wild/
Check out the latest updates on the official *Breath of the Wild* website.

The Legend of Zelda Breath of the Wild - Zelda Wiki
https://zelda.fandom.com/wiki/The_Legend_of_Zelda:_Breath_of_the_Wild
Check out this fan-created guide when you need really detailed *Zelda* information.

INDEX